DANIEL

A STRONG MAN IS FAITHFUL

DANIEL

A STRONG MAN IS FAITHFUL

A 30-DAY DEVOTIONAL

VINCE MILLER

DAVID C COOK
transforming lives together

DANIEL
Published by David C Cook
4050 Lee Vance Drive
Colorado Springs, CO 80918 U.S.A.

Integrity Music Limited, a Division of David C Cook
Brighton, East Sussex BN1 2RE, England

The graphic circle C logo is a registered trademark of David C Cook.

The website addresses recommended throughout this book are offered as a
resource to you. These websites are not intended in any way to be or imply an
endorsement on the part of David C Cook, nor do we vouch for their content.

All Scripture quotations are taken from the ESV® Bible (The Holy Bible,
English Standard Version®), copyright © 2001 by Crossway, a publishing
ministry of Good News Publishers. Used by permission. All rights reserved.
The author has added italics to Scripture quotations for emphasis.

Library of Congress Control Number 2023939766
ISBN 978-0-8307-8624-4
eISBN 978-0-8307-8627-5

The Team: Luke McKinnon, Jeff Gerke, Jack Campbell, Karen Sherry
Cover Design: James Hershberger

Printed in Canada
First Edition 2024

1 2 3 4 5 6 7 8 9 10

102323

CONTENTS

6

CONTENTS

Walking through the Fury 96
He's with You in the Fire 100
Decrees Do Not Change a Nation. 104
God Will Frighten Stubborn Men 108
The Spirit of Babylon Is Here. 111
Here's the Bad News 115
One Last Chance 119
When You Work for a Man Who Thinks He's God 124
God Is Always Speaking. 128
Don't Play God—Just Follow Him 132

To every man facing impossible challenges.
Daniel was faithful from beginning to end.
Be that man.

ABOUT VINCE MILLER

Vince Miller was born in Vallejo, California, and grew up on the West Coast. At twenty, he made a profession of faith while in college and felt a strong, sudden call to work in full-time ministry. After college and graduate school, he invested two decades working with notable ministries like Young Life, InterVarsity Christian Fellowship, the local church, and in senior interim roles. He currently lives in St. Paul, Minnesota, with his wife, Christina, and their three teenage children.

In March 2014, he founded Resolute out of his passion for discipleship and leadership development of men. This passion was born out of his personal need for growth. Vince turned everywhere to find a man who would mentor, disciple, and develop him throughout his spiritual life. He often received one of two answers from well-meaning Christian leaders: either they did not know what to do in a mentoring relationship or they simply did not have the time to do it.

Vince soon learned that he was not alone. Many Christian men were seeking this type of mentoring relationship. Therefore, he felt compelled to build an organization that would focus on ensuring that men who wanted to be discipled would have the opportunity and that mentors would have the tools to disciple other men.

Vince is an authentic and transparent leader who loves to communicate with men and has a deep passion for God's Word. He has authored several books, and he is the primary creator of all Resolute content and training materials.

INTRODUCTION

Daniel is a fascinating character study. His story begins when, as a teen-ager, he is taken into captivity, reeducated, renamed, and possibly castrated. He becomes a refugee in Babylonia under multiple kings, but one in particular—Nebuchadnezzar—looms large in Daniel's story. King Nebuchadnezzar led the greatest superpower nation that had ever existed. He ruled much of the known world.

In this book, we are going to read the compelling account of these two men. In the end, we will learn how to suffer under an enemy king, in a foreign land, underneath unbiblical ideologies, with strange gods, against jealous plots, and before powerful officials—and still remain faithful.

The question I have for you as we begin is: *Are you that man?*

Or maybe the better question is: Do you want to be that man?

If so, you are studying the right book of the Bible, because Daniel is the man to show us the way.

IT'S ALWAYS A SLOW FADE

"In the third year of the reign of Jehoiakim king of Judah,
Nebuchadnezzar king of Babylon came to Jerusalem and
besieged it. And the Lord gave Jehoiakim king of Judah into
his hand, with some of the vessels of the house of God."

Daniel 1:1–2

In these verses, we are confronted with a monumental question: Why did God give his land, people, and leader over to be enslaved by an enemy superpower? We can't ignore Daniel's wording here: "The Lord gave … Judah into his hand."

When we ask a big question of God, we must keep in mind that we might be seeing the situation from a narrow perspective. There is a lot of history that landed Israel in this predicament, and God has a much bigger picture and a longer view of life, events, and people than we do. We see only what we see and draw conclusions from that.

But there are two main reasons why God handed them over. First, he handed them over because God is just. He must discipline his children when they disobey. We don't always like this about God, but he must do this to be true to his character. Second, he handed them over because they were sinful, and he promised he would punish them for their disobedience. Listen to the words of Isaiah:

> Behold, the days are coming, when all that is in your house, and that which your fathers have stored up till this day, shall be carried to Babylon. Nothing shall be left, says the LORD. And some of your own sons, who will come from you, whom you will father, shall be taken away, and they shall be eunuchs in the palace of the king of Babylon. (Isa. 39:6–7)

Sometimes in this life, we don't take God's teachings, directions, and warnings seriously enough. Thus, we distance ourselves from him and his truth to do the things we want to do. As a result, we begin to look more and more like men of the world rather than men of God. And if we become men of the world, then God gives us over to our worldly choices to do what we want to do (see Rom. 1:21–32). God wants a different sort of man for his kingdom.

Sometimes in this life, we don't take God's teachings, directions, and warnings seriously enough.

Paul said in Romans:

> And since they did not see fit to acknowledge God,
> God gave them up to a debased mind to do what ought
> not to be done. (1:28)

As we start our walk through the book of Daniel, be prepared to hear God say some hard things to his nation and people. This means God might have some hard things to say to us and our nation in our time. And remember, he is just, so the time to respond to his discipline is now.

ASK THIS

Are you giving yourself to things that are not of God?

DO THIS

Come back to God today, before he must send strong discipline.

PRAY THIS

God, I come back to you today.

JOURNAL

IT'S ALWAYS A SLOW FADE

ONE FAITHFUL MAN IN UNFAITHFUL TIMES

"In the third year of the reign of Jehoiakim king of Judah,
Nebuchadnezzar king of Babylon came to Jerusalem and
besieged it. And the Lord gave Jehoiakim king of Judah into
his hand, with some of the vessels of the house of God."

Daniel 1:1–2

Yep, same passage as yesterday. But today, I want to highlight the characters, because we need to know them to understand the story.

First, there is Jehoiakim. He was the eighteenth king of Judah. He was not appointed by God but by the Egyptian pharaoh, who politically controlled Judah at the time. Jehoiakim was twenty-five when he became ruler, and he ruled for eleven years. He was described by the biblical authors as a horrific king.

Jewish sources outside the Bible say that he had sex with his mother, daughter-in-law, and stepmother. He murdered men, raped their wives, and stole their property. He had an epispasm (restored foreskin) performed on him to hide that he was a Jew. He is thought to have tattooed his body, which was prohibited by Jewish religious law. But most notably, according to rabbinic tradition, he took a part of a scroll of the Bible, scratched out God's name, and burned it. We might say Jehoiakim was not such a good guy.

Second, we have Nebuchadnezzar. This is actually Nebuchadnezzar II, also known as Nebuchadnezzar the Great. He ruled Babylon for forty-three years, and it was a superpower during his time. Egypt, Israel, and other powers were in decline, but he just kept taking over land and constructing buildings. The city of Babylon became massive and glorious. And that's where the book of Daniel begins. Judah and Jerusalem are in disarray, and God's people are taken captive. And as we read the book, we get to know Nebuchadnezzar more.

Third, there is Daniel. He is unmentioned in these verses, but this book is about his life. Daniel was a teenager when he was captured, and he became a refugee in Babylonia. In the following chapters, we are going to get an overview of his life and prophecies. What is great about this book is that, though Daniel's tale is one of captivity, he remained faithful from beginning to end—all eighty-plus years of his life.

> Though Daniel's tale is one of captivity, he remained faithful from beginning to end.

So right from the start, we have images of three notable men: an unfaithful king of Judah, a pagan enemy king of Babylon, and a man who worships the only King. The contrast between the three is stunning.

But Daniel remains faithful. He outlives and outlasts them both. He is the model of a godly man in unfaithful times. And he will show us and others the way.

ASK THIS

Are you struggling to understand how to be more faithful in faithless times? In what ways?

DO THIS

Resolve to be like Daniel.

PRAY THIS

God, give me wisdom and courage like you did for Daniel.

JOURNAL

ONE FAITHFUL MAN IN UNFAITHFUL TIMES

_____

_____

_____

_____

_____

_____

_____

_____

_____

_____

_____

_____

_____

_____

_____

_____

_____

_____

_____

_____

_____

_____

_____

_____

_____

_____

_____

_____

_____

_____

WHEN GOD TAKES YOU FROM ONE PLACE TO THE NEXT

"And he brought them to the land of Shinar, to the house of
his god, and placed the vessels in the treasury of his god."

Daniel 1:2

Did you notice the beginning of this part of verse 2? It starts with *"And
he brought."* Who was the *he* doing the bringing? It turns out that the *he*
doing the bringing was God. As we noted two days ago in the previous
verses, God was doing the giving. Thus, we must conclude that he was
also doing the bringing here.

Now, certainly, it was Nebuchadnezzar putting the items in his
temple. God wasn't doing that part. And though the king of Babylon
was the instrument used to carry the people into exile, it was God who
was giving Jehoiakim, Jerusalem, the people, and the vessels over to an
enemy nation and king.

Nebuchadnezzar may have believed that he was doing it all, but
Daniel didn't feel this way, nor did he tell the story this way. Do you
know why? Because a redeemed man who lives by a biblical worldview
knows that God is behind all things. A strong man is faithful to believe
this, and he is entirely comfortable with God being in charge.

And look where God brought them. To Shinar. Do you know where this was? It was an infamous Old Testament location. You can read about it in Genesis 11:1–9. The Tower of Babel was constructed in a plain in the land of Shinar.

Think about that for a minute. God took his people from the glory of the Holy City, the location of the Temple of God, and handed them into captivity inside the nation of Babylonia and its impenetrable walled capital city of Babylon, which was near where the Tower of Babel was or had been. Ancient estimates of Babylon's walls say they were eighty-five feet wide, forty feet tall, and as much as sixty miles around. Inside this colossal complex, God's people would be enslaved for the next seventy years.

Interesting, isn't it?

> A strong man is faithful
> to believe this, and he is
> entirely comfortable with
> God being in charge.

Given the tides of change in our culture, don't you wonder how long it might be until God brings *us* into seasons just like these?

In Israel's change of circumstance, we learn two things. First, God is always in control, regardless of the challenges we face. Second, he is looking for faithful men everywhere, whether we live in Jerusalem or

Babylonia, so to speak. The question I have for you today is this: *Are you that man, and do you trust that kind of God?*

ASK THIS

Are you putting your hope in God and his salvation?

DO THIS

Put all your hope in God today.

PRAY THIS

God, I don't trust in anything but you!

JOURNAL

WHEN GOD TAKES YOU FROM ONE PLACE TO THE NEXT

_____

_____

_____

_____

_____

_____

_____

_____

_____

_____

_____

_____

_____

_____

_____

_____

_____

_____

_____

_____

_____

_____

_____

_____

_____

THE BATTLE AGAINST CULTURAL INDOCTRINATION

"Then the king commanded Ashpenaz, his chief eunuch,
to bring some of the people of Israel, both of the royal
family and of the nobility, youths without blemish, of
good appearance and skillful in all wisdom, endowed with
knowledge, understanding learning, and competent to
stand in the king's palace, and to teach them the
literature and language of the Chaldeans. The king
assigned them a daily portion of the food that the king
ate, and of the wine that he drank. They were to be
educated for three years, and at the end of that time
they were to stand before the king."

Daniel 1:3–5

Meet Ashpenaz, lead official of the royal household. We learn two things about him in this passage. First, he was a eunuch, which means he had been castrated. (And let's be clear about what this means. It means his testicles had been removed.) This served to protect the royal court, primarily because he served in a house where he was in the presence of many women, such as the queen, daughters of the king, concubines, and maidservants. Second, he was tasked with choosing the best and bright-est of the exiles from Israel to stand in the king's court.

Notice the list of qualifications for the young men. They had to be:

- without deformity
- handsome
- intelligent, well-trained, and quick to learn

Notice what Nebuchadnezzar did when he got the finest young men the captives have to offer: He indoctrinated them. He reeducated them. Over three years, he would give them the "royal privilege" of learning about Babylonian history, culture, language, and practices in hopes that he might turn them into sympathizers. This was not free education—it was indoctrination by force of people who could not critically challenge the king's "generosity." The plan was to assimilate captive Israelites who would then persuade the rest of Israel.

The same is happening in our time. We have a few powerful entities that control the narrative and are constantly attempting to indoctrinate us. Let's be clear about who is doing this: it's political powers, social media enterprises, large corporations, and media companies with plat-forms and power. And they go after the young and teachable, just like Nebuchadnezzar did.

This is why we must remain in God's Word, especially in these sea-sons of increased rhetoric. We must get our minds, hearts, and souls into the Word of God. It's the only book that has the truth. As the writer of Hebrews stated:

For the word of God is living and active, sharper than any two-edged sword, piercing to the division of soul and of spirit, of joints and of marrow, and discerning the thoughts and intentions of the heart. (4:12)

We must remain in God's Word, especially in these seasons of increased rhetoric.

By investing time in God's Word today, you are becoming a sharper, more discerning, and more intentional man of God.

ASK THIS

Are you letting God's Word define the truth?

DO THIS

Let God's Word determine truth.

PRAY THIS

God, fill my mind with your truth.

JOURNAL

THE BATTLE AGAINST CULTURAL INDOCTRINATION

LIVING IN A WORLD THAT REIDENTIFIES MEN

"Among these were Daniel, Hananiah, Mishael, and
Azariah of the tribe of Judah. And the chief of the
eunuchs gave them names: Daniel he called Belteshazzar,
Hananiah he called Shadrach, Mishael he called Meshach,
and Azariah he called Abednego."

Daniel 1:6–7

The next thing Ashpenaz did was rename these four boys. Let's look at their original names and their meanings, and then their new names and their meanings.

Daniel's name means "God is my judge." He was renamed Belteshazzar, which means "Bel (a Babylonian god) protects his life."

Hananiah. His name means "God has acted graciously." He was renamed Shadrach, which means "Aku (the Babylonian moon god) commands."

Mishael. His name means "There is no god like God." He was renamed Meshach, which means "Aku (the Babylonian moon god) is who god is."

Azariah. His name means "God has helped." He was renamed Abednego, which means "Nabu (a Babylonian god) is god." (By the way, this is the same god that King Nebuchadnezzar is named for. His name means "Nabu protect my eldest son.")

Hopefully, you see what Ashpenaz was doing. He was not only renaming these young men but also intentionally removing God's name. He was trying to remove it from their identity and spoken language. And they were being given new names tied to Babylonian gods. This was the first move of indoctrination—the complete removal of the name of God.

And we do the same thing in our time. Humanity still craves the divine power to control and reidentify ourselves and others through indoctrination. Our sins are no different from those of Ashpenaz and Nebuchadnezzar in Babylonia. We have already taken steps to remove God from our culture and to assign our own identities, genders, and titles. What is happening in our day is just another manifestation of our attempt to play God.

But it's a futile attempt. Because, we can change the calendar to read Common Era (CE), yet most people still know that Jesus is at the center of every date on our calendar. We can remove prayer from schools, yet we still turn to God in times of tragedy within a school. We could even remove "in God we trust" from our money, yet believers would still know that it's only God who can be trusted and only he who has any value.

This is because removing God's name does not remove God. If God is God, then he will not be stopped. And he is looking for faithful men like Daniel, Hananiah, Mishael, and Azariah who will be faithful to his name in culturally combative times.

Are you such a man?

Removing God's name does not remove God.

ASK THIS

Are you such a man as Daniel, Hananiah, Mishael, and Azariah?

DO THIS

Be God's man today. Believe, have faith, and trust only in him.

PRAY THIS

God, give me more faith to trust in you today.

A STRONG MAN MAKES RESOLUTE CHOICES

"But Daniel resolved that he would not defile himself with
the king's food, or with the wine that he drank. Therefore
he asked the chief of the eunuchs to allow him not to
defile himself. And God gave Daniel favor and
compassion in the sight of the chief of the eunuchs."

Daniel 1:8–9

Today's devotional is the first of three that will carry us through the rest of the narrative in Daniel chapter 1. I am going to build the message around the first three words in this text, *"But Daniel resolved."* In this story, we will learn how a strong man does three things: How he makes choices. How he approaches challenges. And how he affects others.

Today is part one—how a strong man makes choices.

A little context will help us here. Daniel was nine hundred miles from his home. He had been taken into captivity, but he was given the royal treatment. He was afforded the best living situation, trained by the best teachers, and fed the best food. Or so it would seem.

The first challenge Daniel encountered was what was on the menu. While the food and drink were fit for a king, Daniel had a twofold problem with the meal plan. First, some of the meat served in the Babylonian palace was pork and venison, unclean animals according to the Mosaic Law. Second, all food and drink was first offered sacrificially to Babylonian gods. Thus, eating that food was understood as worship of those gods.

So, in his first days, Daniel faced a real problem. He could choose to cower in captivity, breaking the Lord's dietary laws to blend in, or he could challenge courageously. Daniel, as we see, chose the latter.

Men face predicaments like this all the time. We find ourselves in situations that urge us to compromise our biblical values. It could be that we are pressured by the agenda of a leader who opposes our faith. Or we could be alone in a compromising position where we are free to act contrary to our beliefs. Or we might feel relational pressure not to act because it might put someone else in danger.

I think Daniel felt all these things. He felt the pressure of an influential leader, the freedom of compromising a situation, and the urge not to act because doing so might put his friends at risk. But Daniel still made the strong choice. I believe he decided that it was better to stay on the right side of the justice of God, even if it meant suffering at the hands of the unjust.

Daniel felt the pressure but still made the strong choice.

I want to encourage you today to be more resolute in every decision you make. Start by making small, strong choices, so that when you get to the big ones, they are easier to make. Then you will know the courage of Daniel.

ASK THIS

What strong choice do you need to make today?

DO THIS

Make it right now. Decide in mind and action.

PRAY THIS

God, I choose to be strong and to make resolute choices.

JOURNAL

A STRONG MAN MAKES RESOLUTE CHOICES

HOW A STRONG MAN
APPROACHES CHALLENGES

"The chief of the eunuchs said to Daniel, 'I fear my lord the
king, who assigned your food and your drink; for why should
he see that you were in worse condition than the youths
who are of your own age? So you would endanger my head
with the king.' Then Daniel said to the steward whom the
chief of the eunuchs had assigned over Daniel, Hananiah,
Mishael, and Azariah, 'Test your servants for ten days; let
us be given vegetables to eat and water to drink. Then let
our appearance and the appearance of the youths who eat
the king's food be observed by you, and deal with your
servants according to what you see.' So he listened to them
in this matter, and tested them for ten days. At the end of
ten days it was seen that they were better in appearance
and fatter in flesh than all the youths who ate the king's
food. So the steward took away their food and the wine
they were to drink, and gave them vegetables."

Daniel 1:10–16

As we said yesterday, this devotional is part of a three-part series where
we learn how a strong man does three things: makes choices, approaches
challenges, and affects others.

Today is part two—how a strong man approaches challenges.

Yesterday, we saw that Daniel made the courageous choice to stand for his biblical convictions. But now he was required to act. And how he approached the challenge would shape the outcome of his conviction.

I believe godly men always feel these spiritual convictions. This is because the Spirit is always convicting—that's his job. But our response to this conviction makes all the difference. There are two extreme responses. The first extreme is the man who acts on the conviction immediately, but his overly passionate approach leaves devastation in his path. Thus, he and others suffer. The second extreme is the man who hesitates to act on the conviction, and his passivity leaves destruction in his path. Thus, he and others suffer.

Let's be honest: You and I have been on both extremes. We have done this at home, work, school, and church, and it results in situations that don't play out well. Our attempt at becoming strong men is foiled because of how passionately—or how slowly—we acted.

But Daniel provided a superior model. He demonstrated how strong men approach a challenge. He was convicted and determined. A step must be taken quickly so passivity won't set in. At the same time, his actions could not be overly passionate or impulsive, or he would endanger himself and others. So Daniel was respectful and tactful, and he presented a solution.

He showed respect by speaking to his superior directly about his conviction. He went privately because he knew his conviction could be interpreted as disrespectful. To reject the provision of the king was to reject the king. And so, Daniel, while passionate, had to regulate his passion.

I think a lot of strong men forget this. We believe our passion gives us the right to be disrespectful. But it doesn't. It is possible to take a hard stand for our views without hating on people. We can be passionately in favor of something, strongly disagree with those on the other side, and yet still speak to them respectfully.

Daniel was tactful and spoke up about his conviction. He couldn't be passive. He had to verbalize his beliefs, even if it cost him his life. So he made them known, not just to his three buds, but also to the person who had the power to initiate the needed change. And he presented them diplomatically. He took a stand but spoke in a way that would encourage Ashpenaz to listen.

> It is possible to take a hard stand for our views without hating on people.

If you tend toward passivity, you may need to tactfully speak up to the right person and stop holding it in.

Further, Daniel also presented a solution. He was in a predicament, but he knew his request would present a dilemma for his superior. So instead of just describing a problem, he offered a solution—a substitute meal plan. Thankfully, it worked. A strong man presents a real solution to the challenge he's facing.

Daniel gives us an incredible example of how to approach challenges resolutely by being respectful, tactful, and solution oriented. And guess what? Everyone wins in this situation. Daniel. Ashpenaz. Nebuchadnezzar. Even the three friends.

Now, this is not guaranteed to work every time. There are plenty of instances when strong men approached a challenge in a good way and yet were stoned, crucified, or beheaded. I can think of a few examples of this in the New Testament. But that doesn't change the fact that what Daniel did was right. Be respectful. Be tactful. Be solution oriented. Be resolute. Be strong.

ASK THIS

What situation do you need to approach differently today?

DO THIS

How could you display respect and tact and offer a solution? Write it down, and then do it.

PRAY THIS

God, win the battle for me today. It belongs to you.

JOURNAL

HOW A STRONG MAN APPROACHES CHALLENGES

_____

_____

_____

_____

_____

_____

_____

_____

_____

_____

_____

_____

_____

_____

_____

_____

_____

_____

_____

_____

_____

_____

_____

HOW A STRONG MAN AFFECTS OTHERS

"As for these four youths, God gave them learning and skill in all literature and wisdom, and Daniel had understanding in all visions and dreams. At the end of the time, when the king had commanded that they should be brought in, the chief of the eunuchs brought them in before Nebuchadnezzar. And the king spoke with them, and among all of them none was found like Daniel, Hananiah, Mishael, and Azariah. Therefore they stood before the king. And in every matter of wisdom and understanding about which the king inquired of them, he found them ten times better than all the magicians and enchanters that were in all his kingdom."

Daniel 1:17–20

This devotion is the third in a three-part series exploring how a strong man does three things: makes choices, approaches challenges, and affects others.

Today is part three—how a strong man affects others.

Strong men understand that every decision they make may affect someone else. But sometimes, the effects of our choices can put others in a real bind. For example, in Daniel's situation, making the best moral choice put three groups of people in danger. First, it put the political authorities over him in a dire situation. Superiors like the chief eunuch were at risk of losing their heads for making a unilateral change to the king's menu. Second, it endangered his three friends. By association with Daniel and his proposal, Hananiah, Mishael, and Azariah (Shadrach, Meshach, and Abednego) were at risk.

Third, we often forget that Daniel's decision also put the other Jewish captives—the ones who were compromising their dietary laws—in a precarious spot. Remember, many other Israelites in Babylon chose not to take this moral stand. Depending on how the whole situation panned out, it could have a deadly impact on them.

> Strong men understand that every decision they make may affect someone else.

Being strong and resolute men means we assess the risks and act, understanding that every important decision and nondecision affects these three groups: authorities, friends, and those who make choices that are different from ours. But we must remain strong, knowing and trusting God. Remember that taking the moral high road may affect others, but its end is always better.

The question for you today is this: Are you affecting others, or are they affecting you?

ASK THIS

What decision will you make today that could have a moral effect on others?

DO THIS

Be strong and resolute.

PRAY THIS

God, may everything I do and say impact others in the way you want it to.

JOURNAL

HOW A STRONG MAN AFFECTS OTHERS

IMPOSSIBLE SITUATIONS ARE POSSIBLE WITH GOD

"In the second year of the reign of Nebuchadnezzar,
Nebuchadnezzar had dreams; his spirit was troubled,
and his sleep left him. Then the king commanded
that the magicians, the enchanters, the sorcerers,
and the Chaldeans be summoned to tell the king his
dreams. So they came in and stood before the king.
And the king said to them, 'I had a dream, and my
spirit is troubled to know the dream.'"

Daniel 2:1–3

We dream all the time. The average person dreams three to five times each night. Most of the time, we don't recall these dreams. We still don't fully understand why we see images in our sleep or the meaning behind them. But popular theories suggest we dream to consolidate memories, process emotions, or clarify desires we may have.

I don't know about you, but I've had seasons of my life that have been troubled by many dreams. They tend to happen when my anxiety is high, and my dreams become more vivid and memorable.

That was Nebuchadnezzar's experience here. He was having very vivid dreams. Therefore, his spirit was troubled, and it prevented him from sleeping.

We know that God gave Nebuchadnezzar these dreams. Perhaps God troubled him with ideas and images that seemed so real that he knew they must have a divine meaning. What the king wanted from his seers was not only the meaning of the dream—he also wanted them to tell him *what* he dreamed, because he himself couldn't remember. That was an impossible order.

Have you ever been in a situation where someone projected their anxiety onto you, hoping you could solve a problem they couldn't? I have. Every day, I talk to some man who finds himself in an impossible predicament, and he comes to me with a problem I cannot solve. Marriage in a mess. Career in chaos. Family in ruin. Overwhelming addictions. I feel the weight of these projected anxieties. More than anything, I would love to remove his anxiety and repair the situation so he can find peace, but I can't.

But there is one thing I can do: I can pray for him. I can bring his impossible situation to the God of the possible.

So today, if you feel you are facing an impossible situation, invite a brother to pray for you. Call, text, or email him, and ask him to shout up a prayer for you. Bring your impossible nightmare and all its anxiety to a God who makes everything possible.

> But Jesus looked at them and said, "With man this is impossible, but with God all things are possible." (Matt. 19:26)

—— I can pray for him. I can bring
his impossible situation to
the God of the possible. ——

ASK THIS

What impossible situation do you need to bring
to God today?

DO THIS

Ask someone to pray for you today.

PRAY THIS

God, I bring this to you today ...

JOURNAL

IMPOSSIBLE SITUATIONS ARE POSSIBLE WITH GOD

GOD IS LOOKING
FOR DANIELS

"Then the Chaldeans said to the king in Aramaic, 'O king, live forever! Tell your servants the dream, and we will show the interpretation.' The king answered and said to the Chaldeans, 'The word from me is firm: if you do not make known to me the dream and its interpretation, you shall be torn limb from limb, and your houses shall be laid in ruins. But if you show the dream and its interpretation, you shall receive from me gifts and rewards and great honor. Therefore show me the dream and its interpretation.' They answered a second time and said, 'Let the king tell his servants the dream, and we will show its interpretation.' The king answered and said, 'I know with certainty that you are trying to gain time, because you see that the word from me is firm—if you do not make the dream known to me, there is but one sentence for you. You have agreed to speak lying and corrupt words before me till the times change. Therefore tell me the dream, and I shall know that you can show me its interpretation.' The Chaldeans answered the king and said, 'There is not a man on earth who can meet the king's demand, for no great and powerful king has asked such a thing of any magician or enchanter or Chaldean. The thing that the king asks is difficult, and no one can show it to the king except the gods, whose dwelling is not with flesh.'"

Daniel 2:4–11

The king had foreseen a powerful image that had troubled him. It could even mean disaster for the kingdom. To get to the bottom of it, he gathered all the seers and diviners.

This monarch was determined and vindictive, so he expedited the process with a twofold promise: either his advisers would be pulled apart limb from limb and suffer the complete destruction of their homes (if they failed) or they would be showered with gifts, rewards, and great honor (if they succeeded). And all that was needed was a single man who could tell him his dream and its meaning.

When men are cornered, we do interesting things, don't we? When we get ambushed by an impossible situation, we will do anything to relieve ourselves from the anxiety of that situation. Occasionally, like Nebuchadnezzar, we project this anxiety onto others, hoping to find a solution. Sometimes, these people cannot bear this burden or find a path to the solution.

When this happens, we discover one important truth: only God can save. And usually, God is looking for an available man to be a vessel to communicate his vision and plan. Daniel was going to be that man.

God is always looking for such men. In every time, culture, family, workplace, and church, he seeks men who will be vessels of his vision and plan. Not your vision and plan. *God's* vision and his plan.

Right now, more than ever, we need men who are available and perched for this moment in time. We need men who are in touch with God, his Word, and his vision for this age. Men who are willing to risk reputation, career, and even life and limb by stepping into the challenge of interpreting the truth and presenting it as it is. This is not a time for timid men—it's a time to speak the truth in a loving way and leave the results to God.

> We need men who are in touch with God, his Word, and his vision for this age.

So, if you feel cornered today, I want to encourage you to seek God's truth. Search his Word for divine direction. If you need help, ask a man of God for advice and direction. Receive his instruction. Do not reject it. And then, when your time comes to speak, do it. Find the most loving and honest way to say it to those who have cornered you. Do not hold back, as intimidating as it may be. You might be the man whom God has chosen for them today.

ASK THIS

Which man are you? The cornered man, like Nebuchadnezzar? Or the Daniel whom someone needs to hear from today?

DO THIS

Remember, God alone can save.

PRAY THIS

God, save me and use me to bring others to your salvation.

JOURNAL

GOD IS LOOKING FOR DANIELS

FAITH PRECEDES
PRESENT ANSWERS

"Because of this the king was angry and very
furious, and commanded that all the wise men of
Babylon be destroyed. So the decree went out,
and the wise men were about to be killed; and they
sought Daniel and his companions, to kill them.
Then Daniel replied with prudence and discretion
to Arioch, the captain of the king's guard, who had
gone out to kill the wise men of Babylon. He
declared to Arioch, the king's captain, 'Why is the
decree of the king so urgent?' Then Arioch made
the matter known to Daniel. And Daniel went in
and requested the king to appoint him a time, that
he might show the interpretation to the king."

Daniel 2:12–16

What I think is interesting about this text is Daniel's response. He had
just gotten word of the situation, and as a reader, I expect him to be terrified. Who wouldn't be frightened by the king's rampage, the orders
given to Arioch, and the life-threatening stress of that moment? But the
text conveys an unusual confidence for a teenager. Daniel approached the

matter with prudence and discretion and asked for an appointment with the king, *even though he didn't know the dream or its interpretation.*

This is the uncomfortable thing about faith in God: faith precedes present answers. Also, sometimes the exercise of faith will put us in harm's way. As we see here, Daniel didn't know the outcome. He didn't know the dream or the interpretation. Yet he took a step of faith, set a meeting with an angry king, and put himself out there, believing that his God was greater than all other gods—and that God would prove himself. Daniel's responsibility was to act in faith; nothing more.

What about you? Are you a man who lives by the sort of faith that makes you willing to trust God and put yourself in harm's way without knowing all the answers?

Faith precedes present answers.

At some point, we are all tested, just like Daniel was. When this moment comes, we will be given the choice to take a safe road or a dangerous one. We will be given the opportunity to trust in ourselves or turn to faith in God.

When a miracle is needed, it's best to remember that faith precedes present answers. But this motivation is not an attempt to put God to the test or manufacture a miracle. Instead, it's living by faith and letting God do what he does best—providing impossible solutions to impossible problems.

ASK THIS

Is there a place where you need to have faith
in God today?

DO THIS

Take a brave step of faith into the unknown.
And let God be God.

PRAY THIS

God, be the God of my situation.

JOURNAL

FAITH PRECEDES PRESENT ANSWERS

IF YOU NEED A MIRACLE, YOU NEED THIS

"Then Daniel went to his house and made the matter known
to Hananiah, Mishael, and Azariah, his companions, and told
them to seek mercy from the God of heaven concerning
this mystery, so that Daniel and his companions might not
be destroyed with the rest of the wise men of Babylon. Then
the mystery was revealed to Daniel in a vision of the night.
Then Daniel blessed the God of heaven."

Daniel 2:17–19

Daniel found himself in a very stressful situation. Sometimes, stress results from sin and selfishness. At other times, stress results from taking a step of faith with God. Personally, I experience more stress from the former than the latter.

But that was not the case here. By faith, Daniel had inserted himself into a unique—but highly stressful—moment. One that only God could resolve. He returned to his home and gathered his friends, and they prayed relentlessly for two things: mercy from God and that he would reveal the mystery of the dream. Daniel knew there were no other means to resolve this issue. If God didn't give mercy, they were all doomed.

I often wonder if we don't see God's greatness more often because we try to do most things ourselves. We can trust our strength, ingenuity, strategy, ability, and talents more than God. We think we'll take that scary step to trust only when we have first saved, prepared, or trained enough. But when we respond this way, we are demonstrating that we're trusting ourselves more than God. We're attempting to reduce the leap of faith to only a reasonable step. And in the end, we miss out on the great things God wants to do for us.

In contrast, Daniel took a massive leap of faith. It was a jump beyond human reach. He did not do this to put God to the test. Instead, he was being faithful. And because he did so, God did something extraordinary. He extended mercy and revealed to Daniel the dream and its meaning.

> I often wonder if we don't see God's greatness more often because we try to do most things ourselves.

I believe God wants to do stuff like this in our time. He wants to use men like us in homes, workplaces, and churches around this country and the world. But we must be humble. We need to be praying. We need to seek God's mercy. And we must start taking some leaps of faith.

Brother, where do you need to take a leap of faith today?

ASK THIS

Where do you need to take a leap of faith today?

DO THIS

Leap.

PRAY THIS

God, as I leap in faith, be faithful.

JOURNAL

IF YOU NEED A MIRACLE, YOU NEED THIS

_____
_____
_____
_____
_____
_____
_____
_____
_____
_____
_____
_____
_____
_____
_____
_____
_____
_____
_____
_____
_____
_____
_____
_____

BUILDING SPIRITUAL CONFIDENCE

"Therefore Daniel went in to Arioch, whom the king
had appointed to destroy the wise men of Babylon.
He went and said thus to him: 'Do not destroy the
wise men of Babylon; bring me in before the king,
and I will show the king the interpretation.'"

Daniel 2:24

Daniel said, "Stop what you're doing. Take me to the king. I will explain the dream."

Don't you love this bring-me-to-the-king moment? I do.

This was not self-confidence—it was confidence in God. Sometimes God-fearing men misunderstand this. The more time we, as God's men, spend in Scripture, the more our minds adjust to a biblical worldview. With this mindset, we begin to see things more clearly, and as we do, we develop more confidence.

But this presents a unique challenge for the Christian man. The danger is in assuming that the wisdom we have gained is something we can use for personal advantage. If we do this, godly confidence becomes self-confidence, which is a move against God.

We can clearly see, by what happened next, that Daniel's bring-me-to-the-king confidence was not self-confidence.

> Then Arioch brought in Daniel before the king in haste and said thus to him: "I have found among the exiles from Judah a man who will make known to the king the interpretation." The king declared to Daniel, whose name was Belteshazzar, "Are you able to make known to me the dream that I have seen and its interpretation?" Daniel answered the king and said, "No wise men, enchanters, magicians, or astrologers can show to the king the mystery that the king has asked, but there is a God in heaven who reveals mysteries, and he has made known to King Nebuchadnezzar what will be in the latter days. Your dream and the visions of your head as you lay in bed are these: To you, O king, as you lay in bed came thoughts of what would be after this, and he who reveals mysteries made known to you what is to be. But as for me, this mystery has been revealed to me, not because of any wisdom that I have more than all the living, but in order that the interpretation may be made known to the king, and that you may know the thoughts of your mind. (Dan. 2:25–30)

Did you hear that? Daniel clarified that "no wise men, enchanters, magicians, or astrologers" could reveal the mystery, but only God in heaven could. He added, "This mystery has been revealed to me, not because of any wisdom that I have." While Daniel was 100 percent confident that he had the answers the king sought, he knew this insight and wisdom were not things he possessed. He was simply a steward, and his confidence was in God. His task was to introduce this great king to the greatest King of all.

What's so ironic about this moment is that, though Nebuchadnezzar had removed God's name from Daniel's name, God took some remarkable steps to make his name known to Nebuchadnezzar.

We need more men like Daniel in our time. Men with steady confidence in God. Men who will take steps of faith. Men who will not let their selfish motives persuade them to use God's wisdom or gifts for personal advantage.

So, here is my question for you today: Is there a place in life today where you need to give credit to God?

If so, give it to him. This is how you build lasting godly confidence.

We need more men like Daniel in our time. Men with steady confidence in God.

ASK THIS

Is there a place in life today where you need to give credit to God?

DO THIS

Give him the credit and build godly confidence.

PRAY THIS

God, you deserve all glory and credit for

_____ today.

JOURNAL

BUILDING SPIRITUAL CONFIDENCE

WHEN YOU ARE AT THE
END OF ALL RESOURCES

"You saw, O king, and behold, a great image. This image, mighty and of exceeding brightness, stood before you, and its appearance was frightening. The head of this image was of fine gold, its chest and arms of silver, its middle and thighs of bronze, its legs of iron, its feet partly of iron and partly of clay. As you looked, a stone was cut out by no human hand, and it struck the image on its feet of iron and clay, and broke them in pieces. Then the iron, the clay, the bronze, the silver, and the gold, all together were broken in pieces, and became like the chaff of the summer threshing floors; and the wind carried them away, so that not a trace of them could be found. But the stone that struck the image became a great mountain and filled the whole earth."

Daniel 2:31–35

Two things grab me about this dream. First is the perspective that the king has in it. He pictures himself standing before a giant image. He is amazed and frightened by its size, sparkle, and craftsmanship. Second, the king witnesses a huge stone hurled with such great force at the image that it annihilates it. Did you note the detail of the stone? It's a stone not crafted or launched by human hands. It's made and thrown by someone greater and more powerful than who created the image. And this terrified the king.

God took the most powerful man in the world at that time and planted a dream in his mind that frightened him to the core. A dream, and nothing more, and yet it was so vivid that Nebuchadnezzar was deeply disturbed by it. The irony is that he had nearly unlimited natural and financial resources at his disposal, yet not even all of these put together could help him know or understand his dream.

Sometimes, we are overwhelmed by the complicated situations we face. They feel more like nightmares. They come with a wide array of emotions. When this happens, we feel small. We don't see a way out because we lack something—like an ability or a resource. Yet when godly men face overwhelming moments like these, they remember something: God has all power and authority to do anything he wants at any time.

Does this mean godly men don't feel small? No. I am sure Daniel felt small as he approached the king. But God gave Daniel a resource, knowledge that only God had: the nightmare that plagued the king's mind.

We have two ways we can live. We can trust in natural resources, or we can trust in supernatural resources. At some point, every man will come to the end of his natural resources. You will come to a place where you have no answers, and you will be terrified. If this is true of a king who had everything, then this is definitely going to be true of you.

> We have two ways we can live. We can trust in natural resources, or we can trust in supernatural resources.

But you don't need to worry, because God has limitless supernatural resources. And he is looking for men like you to steward them so that those who don't have them might hear about them and come to know the God who has all things.

If you are terrified about what's ahead of you, seek God. He has the resources you need.

ASK THIS

What is terrifying you today? Write it out.

DO THIS

Ask God right now for his supernatural resources.

PRAY THIS

God, I need _____ today.

JOURNAL

WHEN YOU ARE AT THE END OF ALL RESOURCES

STANDING AGAINST THE ENEMY KING

"This was the dream. Now we will tell the king its
interpretation. You, O king, the king of kings, to whom
the God of heaven has given the kingdom, the power, and
the might, and the glory, and into whose hand he has
given, wherever they dwell, the children of man, the
beasts of the field, and the birds of the heavens, making
you rule over them all—you are the head of gold."

Daniel 2:36–38

At this point, Daniel had relayed through supernatural revelation what King Nebuchadnezzar's dream had been. The king was probably shocked that Daniel could know this, especially to this detail.

But right into this drama, Daniel inserted a reminder: You might be the current reigning emperor of the world, but there is a God who gave you this dream and gave me the ability to tell it to you. He is the God who created the world, distributes power, determines rulers, and both gives and interprets dreams. This was a vital insertion by Daniel.

Daniel's actions here demonstrate the kind of man whom God desires to use. The kind who is unafraid of standing before all spiritual opposition. Nebuchadnezzar was a pagan, enemy king who had overpowered God's nation and taken his people into exile. Yet in what was likely Daniel's first chance to appear before the king, Daniel wasn't vindictive, angry, or on the attack. He didn't curse or insult the king for what he had done. Because Daniel knew this: Nebuchadnezzar didn't do it—God did.

I think sometimes men misunderstand what it means to be called to stand against spiritual opposition. As we take our stand, we must be careful not to stand against God. Daniel modeled how to do this.

Nebuchadnezzar was Daniel's spiritual opposition. But Daniel knew that God brought the nation into exile because of their unfaithfulness. So, Daniel was content to trust God in this situation. Should Daniel have compromised his spiritual beliefs because he was now far away from his homeland, where the rulers of the day would allow such behavior? No. But as Daniel walked new terrain, he needed to find new ways to stand against his opposition. As God's man, he had to be careful not to make compromises as he stood up for his beliefs. He had to be sure that in the process of standing against his opposition, he didn't end up standing against God.

Daniel knew God had given him a supernatural revelation with extraordinary power. But he was careful to steward this in a way that brought attention to God, not himself or his sense of justice. So he spoke into this moment, reminding Nebuchadnezzar that he was great but that there was a greater King.

In a way, I think Daniel might even have been making this statement here to remind the king, and himself, that God was still in charge—so he would not act against God.

As you go about this day, remind yourself that God is still in charge. It may not seem like it, but he's got this. And then, when God calls you to stand against spiritual opposition, go for it. Speak up. But as you do it, be careful not to stand against God, because no man stands against our great God without consequence.

> As you go about this day,
> remind yourself that God
> is still in charge. It may not
> seem like it, but he's got this.

ASK THIS

Where do you need to stand against spiritual opposition?

DO THIS

Stand up and speak out.

PRAY THIS

God, show me how to stand up and speak out. But may I never stand against you.

JOURNAL

STANDING AGAINST THE ENEMY KING

THE NIGHTMARE OF
MORAL DECLINE

"You are the head of gold. Another kingdom inferior to
you shall arise after you, and yet a third kingdom of
bronze, which shall rule over all the earth. And there shall
be a fourth kingdom, strong as iron, because iron breaks
to pieces and shatters all things. And like iron that
crushes, it shall break and crush all these."

Daniel 2:38–40

Daniel finally revealed to the king the meaning of the dream. These verses speak of four great world empires. When Daniel shared this with Nebuchadnezzar, only one of the four existed. But today, looking back over hundreds of years with a greater perspective, we know who all four empires were. God's word came to pass without fail.

First is the Babylonian Empire, represented by the head of gold. Second is the Medo-Persian Empire, represented by the silver chest and arms. The bronze belly and thighs represent the Greek Empire, led by Alexander the Great. Fourth is the Roman Empire, represented by the iron legs (see Dan. 2:32–33).

Though they did not know all the empires foretold in his dream, one thing would have been hard to miss: the slow decline of an empire in dignity, wealth, and strength.

In our time, I think we are still witnessing many of the effects of this dream. Yet because we live many centuries after, we have greater perspective. We have a view of something God did during that fourth-world empire, the Roman Empire. God sent a Savior to this world during this period—his Son, Jesus.

He sent hope into a world that was in aggressive moral decline. And through Jesus, God's perfectly moral Son, all of mankind is given hope. By God's hand of grace, Jesus became the sacrifice for our immorality and sin and gave us hope of being redeemed from the moral decay of this world. He did all the work because we rebelled against him and failed to be moral.

Jesus doesn't expect perfect morality from us, and he doesn't want us to attempt to establish a utopia here on earth. He wants us to have faith in his perfect sacrifice and believe in his resurrection from the dead till we move from this immoral world into a sinless eternity. Until then, we strive to live as strong, faithful, and righteous men in a world in perpetual moral decline.

We strive to live as strong, faithful, and righteous men in a world in perpetual moral decline.

Here is the message we need to proclaim today: The world will decline and come to an end. This means we can live like King Nebuchadnezzar, terrified by this truth, and choose not to turn to God. Or we can choose to imitate Daniel and continue to live by faith through the decline, telling others the truth along the way, hoping they too will turn to God.

Tell someone the truth about Jesus today, before this world and our time come to an end.

ASK THIS

What can you do to continue having faith in a world in moral decline? Write it out.

DO THIS

Tell someone about the faith you have in Jesus.

PRAY THIS

God, give me the courage to tell others about Jesus.

JOURNAL

THE NIGHTMARE OF MORAL DECLINE

ONLY GOD PREDICTS
THE FUTURE

"There shall be a fourth kingdom, strong as iron, because iron breaks to pieces and shatters all things. And like iron that crushes, it shall break and crush all these. And as you saw the feet and toes, partly of potter's clay and partly of iron, it shall be a divided kingdom, but some of the firmness of iron shall be in it, just as you saw iron mixed with the soft clay. And as the toes of the feet were partly iron and partly clay, so the kingdom shall be partly strong and partly brittle. As you saw the iron mixed with soft clay, so they will mix with one another in marriage, but they will not hold together, just as iron does not mix with clay. And in the days of those kings the God of heaven will set up a kingdom that shall never be destroyed, nor shall the kingdom be left to another people. It shall break in pieces all these kingdoms and bring them to an end, and it shall stand forever, just as you saw that a stone was cut from a mountain by no human hand, and that it broke in pieces the iron, the bronze, the clay, the silver, and the gold. A great God has made known to the king what shall be after this. The dream is certain, and its interpretation sure."

Daniel 2:40–45

This was an incredible dream, revelation, and interpretation that God delivered to Daniel and Nebuchadnezzar. It made known thousands of years of future events. No wonder the king was terrified by it. He was given a glimpse far into the future. And get this: Nebuchadnezzar was not a God-fearing man. Many people come in the name of the Lord, thinking they know future events. Yet here, God gave this knowledge to someone who did not know or fear him. God does stuff like this all the time so we will know the expanse of his power.

I think this dream still terrifies men today. As we saw last time, we understand aspects of this prophecy today because history has revealed them. Yet there are other parts we still do not understand. For example, we know who these first four world empires were, but there is much debate about what kingdom the toes and feet represent. However, we can be certain that all world empires will one day end, and God will establish another kingdom—a holy empire.

Isn't this just like our God? He gives us enough detail that we'll know what's happening when it's happening, but not so much that it exempts us from trusting him.

For example, did you know there are hundreds of sacred texts from religions all over the world, spanning thousands of years? Yet only the Bible contains so much specific, detailed prophecy about—and gloriously fulfilled by—a single man: Jesus. This prophecy includes so much detail that I believe it is only explainable if it was disclosed by the one true God.

And right here in Daniel 2, that's what we have: thousands of years of events prophesied in such detail that only God could have revealed them. God consistently proves that only he knows the endgame. That's why all visionaries, prophets, and philosophers are no match for the only true God.

> God gives us enough detail that we'll know what's happening when it's happening, but not so much that it exempts us from trusting him.

God knows the times in which we live. He knows the leaders of this world are losing their minds. But guess what? He's got it all figured out. We must be faithful as he reveals the next portion of the prophecy in our time. One day, he's going to hurl a giant rock at the empires of this world and establish a new empire under a holy and righteous King.

ASK THIS

How are you losing hope given the events of our time and the things of this world? Write it out.

DO THIS

Turn to faith and be faithful.

PRAY THIS

God, rescue us from the events of our time and this failing world.

JOURNAL

ONLY GOD PREDICTS THE FUTURE

DON'T WORSHIP YOURSELF. WORSHIP HIM.

"King Nebuchadnezzar made an image of gold, whose height was sixty cubits and its breadth six cubits. He set it up on the plain of Dura, in the province of Babylon. Then King Nebuchadnezzar sent to gather the satraps, the prefects, and the governors, the counselors, the treasurers, the justices, the magistrates, and all the officials of the provinces to come to the dedication of the image that King Nebuchadnezzar had set up. Then the satraps, the prefects, and the governors, the counselors, the treasurers, the justices, the magistrates, and all the officials of the provinces gathered for the dedication of the image that King Nebuchadnezzar had set up. And they stood before the image that Nebuchadnezzar had set up. And the herald proclaimed aloud, 'You are commanded, O peoples, nations, and languages, that when you hear the sound of the horn, pipe, lyre, trigon, harp, bagpipe, and every kind of music, you are to fall down and worship the golden image that King Nebuchadnezzar has set up. And whoever does not fall down and worship shall immediately be cast into a burning fiery furnace.' Therefore, as soon as all the peoples heard the sound of the horn, pipe, lyre, trigon, harp, bagpipe, and every kind of music, all the peoples, nations, and languages fell down and worshiped the golden image that King Nebuchadnezzar had set up."

Daniel 3:1–7

Let's recap. King Nebuchadnezzar was the king who ruled a swath of the planet. He recently had overpowered Judah and Jerusalem, taking captive some of the best and brightest of God's people. Four young men—whom we know by the names Daniel, Shadrach, Meshach, and Abednego—became the center of the story. They were forced to walk hundreds of miles to the city of Babylon, which is in modern-day Iraq. They were reeducated according to a pagan language and philosophy. Then they might have been physically mutilated by castration, which would've been something more serious than circumcision but not so far as sexual reassignment. To top it off, they were given new names that deleted God's name from their identities.

These occurrences are fascinating, aren't they, given the signs of our times and what we see happening in our culture?

Then Nebuchadnezzar had this terrifying dream and demanded that unless someone could tell him both the dream and the interpretation, he would slay all his magicians and seers. At the last minute, Daniel came forward to tell him about the dream and the interpretation. We then witness what appears to be a reverent king. But don't be fooled: we haven't gotten to chapter 3 yet.

Now we fast-forward about twenty years and find the story recounted in today's passage. Apparently, this king did not have a problem with self-esteem. Who's arrogant enough to build a statue of themselves six stories tall? Yet, lots of monarchs have done similar things. You can find leader shrines today in countries like China and North Korea. But this king went one step further. He gathered his political forces, not for a vote, but to deliver a mandate. He demanded that everyone bow down and worship him, on pain of death. I think it's safe to say that this guy had a little bit of a messiah complex. And you thought your boss was an arrogant narcissist.

We might be prone to think Nebuchadnezzar had lost his mind, but he was merely a depiction of the sinfulness and selfishness in every man's heart. He was a manifestation of how arrogant we all can be. The difference between him and us is that he had the power and wealth to display it shamelessly.

Those of us not leading a monarchy might be better at hiding our desire to possess power and control, but we all have it. We may attempt to grasp these things at work, and we may attempt to do so at home. And if we cannot get enough of it there, we coach youth sports to gain some means of control over others. Laughable, I know, and sad—but I'm guessing you know there's some truth in this.

The problem with this kind of power and control is that it's born from selfish desires and is based on deep, unseen feelings of insecurity. When we're in that place, we demand worship (respect) and hand out harsh punishments when we're not obeyed—which is precisely what Nebuchadnezzar did. Yet this is exactly the opposite of how God behaves. God leads from pure love and true justice, giving a man a choice to obey or disobey so that the worship he does give is freely offered.

Brother, this is why we must daily and regularly worship God. As we worship God, we submit our fears and insecurities to him. We destroy the idols of selfishness and the desire for power and control. So today, confess a selfish desire. Write it out if you so desire, and offer it to God as a sacrifice.

God leads from pure love and
true justice, giving a man a
choice to obey or disobey so
that the worship he does give
is freely offered.

ASK THIS

What desire do you need to sacrifice to God?

DO THIS

Give it to God and worship him.

PRAY THIS

God, you are worthy of all worship.

JOURNAL

DON'T WORSHIP YOURSELF. WORSHIP HIM.

POLICING THE MANDATE

"Therefore at that time certain Chaldeans came forward and maliciously accused the Jews. They declared to King Nebuchadnezzar, 'O king, live forever! You, O king, have made a decree, that every man who hears the sound of the horn, pipe, lyre, trigon, harp, bagpipe, and every kind of music, shall fall down and worship the golden image. And whoever does not fall down and worship shall be cast into a burning fiery furnace. There are certain Jews whom you have appointed over the affairs of the province of Babylon: Shadrach, Meshach, and Abednego. These men, O king, pay no attention to you; they do not serve your gods or worship the golden image that you have set up.'"

Daniel 3:8–12

Yesterday, we learned that Nebuchadnezzar made a ninety-foot-tall golden image of himself and demanded that everyone worship it. Today's passage reveals what happened next.

Basically, you have a group of jealous people policing the king's mandate. I think we get what's happening here because we have all been victimized by government mandates. Or we have supported using them against others.

Such things tend to happen under leadership that demands compliance. The people most prone to be on the attack are those who created the mandate. And those most liable to *be* attacked are those who are not in favor of it.

In this situation, a small group of Chaldeans were keeping a watchful eye on three men—Shadrach, Meshach, and Abednego. The Chaldeans likely had been observing them since Daniel promoted them over all the other advisers to the king (Dan. 2:46–49). The envy over their advancement to higher positions and status motivated the Chaldeans to try to get rid of them. If they couldn't assassinate them outright, maybe they could have them sentenced to death for noncompliance. They desired to exert control over others when they felt out of control.

But while this might get you all worked up, this doesn't happen just within politics and government. It occurs in the church too. Throughout the Gospels and Paul's letters, we read how religious leaders repeatedly attempted to leverage laws and rules to mandate obedience. And guess what: it didn't work. It never works. Do you know why? Because we have rebellious hearts. We are born into this world with a spirit of noncompliance. No dictator, monarch, business leader, manager, authority, or parent can mandate enough laws to change the human heart. The heart, by nature, is noncompliant.

But here's the game changer: once we learn this principle and have been impacted by it enough, we can choose to submit our wayward heart to God willingly, and he can rule over it. Ezekiel 36:26 reads, "And I [the Lord] will give you a new heart, and a new spirit I will put within you."

──── If you are going to resist
authority, make sure you are
not doing so for selfish reasons. ────

Friend, if you have a rebellious spirit, it's possible that it might be partially right and righteous. As we will discover, these three men will resist this mandate for right and righteous reasons. Most of the time, though, a rebellious spirit comes from a desire to control or not be controlled, and this arises for sinful and selfish reasons. Sometimes, deep down, we have trouble admitting to ourselves that this rebellious spirit wants freedom from everything, even the law of God.

If you are going to resist authority, make sure you are not doing so for selfish reasons, because you'll only end up resisting the law of God's grace.

ASK THIS
Where do you have a rebellious spirit right now?

DO THIS
Resist that spirit and call on the Holy Spirit.

PRAY THIS
God, may I resist the spirit of the world but never your Spirit.

JOURNAL

POLICING THE MANDATE

IT'S TIME TO TAKE A STAND

"Then Nebuchadnezzar in furious rage commanded that
Shadrach, Meshach, and Abednego be brought. So they
brought these men before the king. Nebuchadnezzar
answered and said to them, 'Is it true, O Shadrach,
Meshach, and Abednego, that you do not serve my gods
or worship the golden image that I have set up? Now if
you are ready when you hear the sound of the horn, pipe,
lyre, trigon, harp, bagpipe, and every kind of music, to fall
down and worship the image that I have made, well and
good. But if you do not worship, you shall immediately be
cast into a burning fiery furnace. And who is the god who
will deliver you out of my hands?' Shadrach, Meshach,
and Abednego answered and said to the king, 'O
Nebuchadnezzar, we have no need to answer you in this
matter. If this be so, our God whom we serve is able to
deliver us from the burning fiery furnace, and he will
deliver us out of your hand, O king. But if not, be it
known to you, O king, that we will not serve your gods or
worship the golden image that you have set up.'"

Daniel 3:13–18

The king was hacked off at these guys, and for several reasons. First, they
refused to worship his gods. Second, they refused to worship *him*. I think

it's safe to say that Nebuchadnezzar had become a full-blown narcissist. Over the intervening twenty years, he had convinced himself that he was a god and he was worthy of worship. And he believed that no one could save these three men from his godlike vengeance.

But Shadrach, Meshach, and Abednego were going to take a stand. They made two declarations to the king: that God had more power than he did and that worshipping God was more beneficial than worshipping him.

It's important to note that they were not putting God to the test, jumping into a furnace and trying to demand that God save them. They were being faithful regardless of the outcome. I don't think they cared about the outcome at all. In life or death, they were content to go down as men who had been faithful to God in a faithless country.

We must be men like this. But while we might aspire to live like this in our time, we cannot be like these men if we are not taking the daily steps they had taken over the previous twenty years. For two decades of captivity, these three men took steps of obedience in faith that prepared them to face this ultimate test.

In life or death, they were content to go down as men who had been faithful to God in a faithless country.

One day, God may test you like this. It could come sooner than you think. But until then, we need to live every day fully trusting God. Our actions must show that we trust him more than we trust our money, investments, and retirement plan. That we trust him more than our solutions, power, and abilities. That we trust him more than we do any president, politician, or Supreme Court ruling. That we trust him more than a specific outcome in our marriage, family, or career.

Today, you probably won't have to take a stand like these men did. But you can take a small step of faith, believing that God has more power and benefit than anything else you can imagine. As you do that today, know that God might be preparing you for more significant moments just around the bend.

ASK THIS

In what situation do you need to take a stand today, and what action do you need to take?

DO THIS

Take that action today so you can take a stand tomorrow.

PRAY THIS

God, make me a man of great faith.

JOURNAL

IT'S TIME TO TAKE A STAND

WALKING THROUGH THE FURY

"Then Nebuchadnezzar was filled with fury, and the
expression of his face was changed against Shadrach,
Meshach, and Abednego. He ordered the furnace heated
seven times more than it was usually heated. And he
ordered some of the mighty men of his army to bind
Shadrach, Meshach, and Abednego, and to cast them
into the burning fiery furnace. Then these men were
bound in their cloaks, their tunics, their hats, and their
other garments, and they were thrown into the burning
fiery furnace. Because the king's order was urgent and
the furnace overheated, the flame of the fire killed those
men who took up Shadrach, Meshach, and Abednego.
And these three men, Shadrach, Meshach, and
Abednego, fell bound into the burning fiery furnace."

Daniel 3:19–23

I could be wrong, but I think there's almost no chance that I will experience something like this during my lifetime. Yet I do believe we'll all
encounter moments that will frighten us. Moments when we'll feel
powerless and overwhelmed by someone with the upper hand. This
could happen on the job, at home, or in the courtroom. We might be
standing before a boss, a spouse, or a leader.

Most of the time, this happens when we've done something wrong that comes with a penalty. But this moment in Babylon had nothing to do with sin. These men did not sin against God. Instead, they stood up for God, which required them to oppose a king who had proclaimed to be a god. They chose to do what was right and righteous, and they were prepared to suffer for it at the hands of a cruel, self-righteous, and angry king.

Now *that's* something we may experience. We will, or should be willing to, suffer for doing what is right and righteous in this life. I already have suffered at the hands of cruel, self-righteous, and angry men. These men are out there. Today, they are heating things up seven times more than usual.

However, though they are perched at their keyboards and ready with their phones to eviscerate others with their posts and sound bites, we must not back down from our faith in God. Now may be the time for greater faith in a God who might be taking us to the edge of the flame. Sometimes, it's only when the flame of persecution is hottest that we remove all possibility of natural solutions and see the work of a supernatural God.

> We will, or should be willing to, suffer for doing what is right and righteous in this life.

If things are heating up in your life, have faith a little longer. God might be waiting to provide a supernatural solution that turns many toward him.

ASK THIS

What supernatural solution do you need?
Write this out.

DO THIS

Let someone pray for you by sharing with
them what you wrote in response to the
question above.

PRAY THIS

God, give me faith and work supernaturally
through me so your glory might be revealed
to those around me.

JOURNAL

WALKING THROUGH THE FURY

HE'S WITH YOU IN THE FIRE

"King Nebuchadnezzar was astonished and rose up in haste. He declared to his counselors, 'Did we not cast three men bound into the fire? ... But I see four men unbound, walking in the midst of the fire, and they are not hurt; and the appearance of the fourth is like a son of the gods.... Shadrach, Meshach, and Abednego, servants of the Most High God, come out, and come here!' Then Shadrach, Meshach, and Abednego came out from the fire.... The [king's officials] saw that the fire had not had any power over the bodies of those men. The hair of their heads was not singed, their cloaks were not harmed, and no smell of fire had come upon them. Nebuchadnezzar said, 'Blessed be the God of Shadrach, Meshach, and Abednego, who has sent his angel and delivered his servants, who trusted in him, and set aside the king's command, and yielded up their bodies rather than serve and worship any god except their own God.... For there is no other god who is able to rescue in this way.'"

Daniel 3:24–30

Like all men throughout history, we live in times ruled by the spirit of Babylon. Satan roams the earth, and men like Nebuchadnezzar still exist.

They will till the end of time. Therefore, we're going to have trouble in this life. We might have long seasons of fiery trials. Trials in the world, in our countries, with governments, politicians, and leaders. We'll experience trials in our marriages, families, workplaces, and personal lives. Some days, the furnace of these trials is going to rage. Occasionally, the heat will get turned way up.

But know this: a man of faith always has God standing by his side. God will stand by you in the fire when a vengeful spirit walks you to the edge of the furnace and pushes you in. God will be there. It's possible that he will decide to intervene miraculously, not letting you be burned. Not a hair on your body. Not a singe of your skin. Not even a smell of flame. Or else he will simply be with you through it all and on into eternity. That's up to him. Your task is to have faith that the Spirit of God is greater than the spirit of this world.

Write down at least one fiery trial God recused you from. I believe these moments happen more than we know. I believe God is still working miracles and saving men from the trials of this life. So share what God rescued you from, and give hope to men who might be walking through that same fire today.

> Your task is to have faith that the Spirit of God is greater than the spirit of this world.

ASK THIS

What fiery trial has God saved you from or are you in now?

DO THIS

Share your story with another man who may be in the fire.

PRAY THIS

God, give me faith in the fire.

JOURNAL

HE'S WITH YOU IN THE FIRE

DECREES DO NOT CHANGE A NATION

"King Nebuchadnezzar to all peoples, nations, and
languages, that dwell in all the earth: Peace be
multiplied to you! It has seemed good to me to show
the signs and wonders that the Most High God has
done for me. How great are his signs, how mighty his
wonders! His kingdom is an everlasting kingdom, and
his dominion endures from generation to generation."

Daniel 4:1–3

After witnessing the miracle at the furnace, Nebuchadnezzar delivered a decree to his empire. He declared God's greatness, might, and dominion. But don't assume that he was making a confession of faith, because he was not.

What we have here was a narcissistic leader who had seen a miracle and believed that God put on a show for him. Out of respect for the miracle, recognizing three men had just walked into and out of a fiery furnace unharmed, he made a declaration to the nation about what God had done for him. For *him*. Not what God had done for Shadrach, Meshach, and Abednego, but for him.

I think we learn a great lesson here.

Godly decrees by a national leader do not make a God-fearing nation. This type of decree is a declaration and nothing more. Maybe something like a press release or official statement. While decrees can determine a course of action and define consequences, the only thing that makes a decree godly is if it comes from God. It will also fall flat unless the men who hear it are willing to obey.

It's impossible to legislate godliness, because our hearts are recklessly rebellious. We do what we want to do. Our hearts rebel against things we don't like.

Mankind is so creatively rebellious that we'll hate every decree and look for ways around them. You and I are no different. When I even hear a decree, I instinctively look for a way around it.

But there is one thing that makes a godly decree work: a man willing to submit to that decree. If the decree is from God or his representative, we must be willing to surrender to it and to the person who declared it, knowing they have the public interest in mind. This too is a test of our faith: the choice is ours to submit or rebel. God is looking for devotion to him, not half-hearted decrees from half-hearted belief. God is raising up men who are all in for him.

Nebuchadnezzar was not all in. Yes, he made a very noble decree, but he did not show remorse for his sin. He did not change his behavior. He did not believe God was greater than himself or the Babylonian idols. He was not going to submit to God. To him, God was just one of the many gods across his land. So basically, what you have with this decree is nothing but theater. It was a show. It was acting. It was hypocrisy.

> ───── There is one thing that makes a
> godly decree work: a man willing
> to submit to that decree. ─────

God is looking for men to live all in. He is not looking for half-hearted belief. He is looking for men who willingly and wholeheartedly follow him. Is today the day you will make that decision?

ASK THIS

Are you ready to follow God wholeheartedly?

DO THIS

Declare it by writing it down.

PRAY THIS

God, I am ready to go all in with you. Today, I give you everything and trust your every decree.

JOURNAL

DECREES DO NOT CHANGE A NATION

_____

_____

_____

_____

_____

_____

_____

_____

_____

_____

_____

_____

_____

_____

_____

_____

_____

_____

_____

_____

_____

_____

_____

_____

GOD WILL FRIGHTEN
STUBBORN MEN

"I, Nebuchadnezzar, was at ease in my house and
prospering in my palace. I saw a dream that made me
afraid. As I lay in bed the fancies and the visions of my
head alarmed me. So I made a decree that all the wise
men of Babylon should be brought before me, that they
might make known to me the interpretation of the dream.
Then the magicians, the enchanters, the Chaldeans, and
the astrologers came in, and I told them the dream, but
they could not make known to me its interpretation."

Daniel 4:4–7

In this situation, the king shifted suddenly from ease to terror. The text
is very dramatic. In one verse, he was in one state, and in the next, he was
terrified. Once again, it was a dream that caused him to panic.

God can reach any man. There is no man alive who is out of his
reach. God can reach the most stubborn, immovable, arrogant, and resistant man. He can get to him even if he's inside the confines of a fortress,
protected by soldiers and surrounded by aides. He can and will penetrate
his mind with dreams, visions, images, and nightmares. He can do this
anytime and anywhere when he wants to get a man's attention.

In the New Testament, he did it with military commanders like Cornelius, simple followers like Ananias, influential religious leaders like Saul, and faithful disciples like Peter. Right here in today's passage, God reached into the mind of the world's richest and most powerful monarch.

> God can reach the most stubborn, immovable, arrogant, and resistant man. He can get to him even if he's inside the confines of a fortress.

Do you know someone who seems immune to the ways of God? Someone as stubborn as this king? You might pray this simple prayer: "God, would you please awaken their mind to you through a dream?" Sometimes this might be the only way to reach those men who seem unreachable.

ASK THIS
Is there someone you know who is resistant to God?

DO THIS
Write out a prayer for them today.

PRAY THIS
God, reach into the mind of the resistant today. I want them desperately to know you and your ways.

JOURNAL

GOD WILL FRIGHTEN STUBBORN MEN

THE SPIRIT OF
BABYLON IS HERE

"At last Daniel came in before me—he who was named
Belteshazzar after the name of my god, and in whom is
the spirit of the holy gods—and I told him the dream,
saying, 'O Belteshazzar, chief of the magicians, because
I know that the spirit of the holy gods is in you and that
no mystery is too difficult for you, tell me the visions of
my dream that I saw and their interpretation. The visions
of my head as I lay in bed were these: I saw, and behold,
a tree in the midst of the earth, and its height was great.'"

Daniel 4:8–10

Into this baffling moment walked Daniel. He was a man of God living
during some challenging times. He was a captive in a major metropolitan
city. He had been reeducated by leading pagan scholars. Government
legislation seemed bent on trying to force him to participate in heretical
spiritual practices. They had even given him a new name.

Daniel was the overseer of all the magicians, astrologers, and seers in
the land. And he was about to interact with a king who worshipped himself. This king had erected a massive golden statue of himself and

demanded that everyone in his empire worship him. We might say that this empire was possessed by the "spirit of Babylon."

This period is the birthplace of that idea. Babylon is talked about in the Bible in several places, such as the book of Daniel and the book of Revelation. In our modern language, "the spirit of Babylon" describes any corrupt system that works in opposition to the Spirit of God.

If you look back over time, you will readily detect its work. It has been active through nations, governments, philosophies, religions, and individuals. It was present in Sodom and Gomorrah, and in more recent history, we've seen its work through Nazi Germany and North Korea. It is at work through organizations that traffic drugs and humans.

Recently, some have felt they've detected expressions of this spirit in the curriculum taught to our children, the planning behind political narratives, and the media platforms entertaining the minds of our families. The spirit of Babylon has been and always will be all around us.

But then, there was God's man in the middle of it all. He was noticeably different. Even Nebuchadnezzar could detect it in Daniel, saying that "the spirit of the holy gods" was in him. While Daniel was governed by the king of Babylon, reeducated by Babylonian professors, and renamed after a Babylonian god, he remained resolute. He was led by the Spirit of God and remained *in* but not *of* the world.

Our time is becoming more and more like this. We are watching the intentional and systematic expansion of the spirit of Babylon. And what we need today are more men sold out for God than ever before. Men who are led by his Spirit. Invite God's Spirit to give you direction today. Today might be a day you are called to stand before someone overcome by the spirit of Babylon.

> —— The spirit of Babylon has
> been and always will be all
> around us. But God's man
> is in the middle of it all. ——

ASK THIS

Are you being challenged by a spirit of Babylon?

DO THIS

Ask God for strength by the Holy Spirit.

PRAY THIS

God, may your Spirit be with me in every encounter and before all my opposition.

JOURNAL

THE SPIRIT OF BABYLON IS HERE

HERE'S THE BAD NEWS

"Then Daniel, whose name was Belteshazzar, was
dismayed for a while, and his thoughts alarmed him. The
king answered and said, 'Belteshazzar, let not the dream
or the interpretation alarm you.' Belteshazzar answered
and said, 'My lord, may the dream be for those who hate
you and its interpretation for your enemies!'"

Daniel 4:19

Daniel was about to deliver terrible news to his opposition. Remember that this king was politically, religiously, philosophically, and pragmatically opposed to Daniel and his God. This is just a guess, but I think most men in Daniel's situation would be delighted. Finally, he was getting to announce that God was bringing justice to this pagan king. He had, after all, done some awful things to God's people, and he had rejected God.

But the way Daniel stewarded this bad news was notable. We learn from his example how a man of God should approach challenging moments. We read here that he was dismayed and alarmed. He approached this situation with respect and care because he had to deliver the news that Nebuchadnezzar's kingdom was in crisis.

God's man carries tremendous responsibility to deliver both good news and bad news. Everyone loves the good news because it's good. But sometimes, in order to get to the good news, we have to share bad news. In such a case, we must seek to share the bad news in a way that others can know the truth of sin and see hope in God.

I think Daniel felt the weight of this stewardship, and that was why he was dismayed and alarmed. He was not just afraid of how Nebuchadnezzar might respond (though that's big, because kings often get in murderous moods when given really bad news), but he was also experiencing a reverent fear of a message from God that he had been called to steward.

> God's man carries tremendous responsibility to deliver both good news and bad news.

You and I live in a world that needs both good news and bad news. So, charge into it with a reverent fear that God will bring you into someone's life to deliver those messages. When that moment comes, making you tremble, say what God is calling you to say. And don't make it about you. It's not your message. It's God's. All of it. Both the good and the bad. It's what he is going to use to point the person to him.

ASK THIS

Who is a person you need to tell the truth to today?

DO THIS

Write that person's name, and write out the message you need to share.

PRAY THIS

God, it's your message, not mine. May I say it your way, not mine.

JOURNAL

HERE'S THE BAD NEWS

ONE LAST CHANCE

"The tree you saw, which grew and became strong, so
that its top reached to heaven, and it was visible to the
end of the whole earth ... it is you, O king.... Your
greatness has grown and reaches to heaven, and your
dominion to the ends of the earth. And because the king
saw a watcher, a holy one, coming down from heaven and
saying, 'Chop down the tree and destroy it, but leave the
stump of its roots in the earth, bound with a band of iron
and bronze, in the tender grass of the field, and let him be
wet with the dew of heaven, and let his portion be with
the beasts of the field, till seven periods of time pass over
him,' this is the interpretation, O king: It is a decree of
the Most High, which has come upon my lord the king,
that you shall be driven from among men, and your
dwelling shall be with the beasts of the field.... You shall
be wet with the dew of heaven, and seven periods of time
shall pass over you, till you know that the Most High rules
the kingdom of men and gives it to whom he will. And as
it was commanded to leave the stump of the roots of the
tree, your kingdom shall be confirmed for you from the
time that you know that Heaven rules. Therefore, O king
... break off your sins by practicing righteousness, and
your iniquities by showing mercy to the oppressed, that
there may perhaps be a lengthening of your prosperity."

Daniel 4:20–27

This interpretation is interesting. While this was a historical event, it's also a parable of how most men live. We start by trying to do it our way, with us in the leaders' seats. Eventually, we realize that our way doesn't work or isn't going to work forever. Then we come to a moment of decision: either we're the leaders of our lives or God is. Because there cannot be two leaders in my life. He's the king of my life or I am. He's the Lord of my life or I am. He's the Savior of my life or I am.

Right at the end of the interpretation, Daniel offered the king some free advice: repent. He essentially said, "My king, I have walked with you for thirty years. You have gained it all. The world is at your command. However, because you are not a god, you will die one day. But you can know one. He is the one true God, the highest and only God. He gave you this dream to warn you to stop sinning and to start living righteously. So why not turn to him and spend this last part of your life even better than the first? Perhaps this future can be delayed or even avoided."

Here are two actionables:

First, if you are a man who wants to live the last part of your life better than the first, I want you to know you can declare that right now. You can surrender your life to God today and proclaim him the leader of your life; I will pray you through it. Just visit this webpage or follow the QR code below: https://beresolute.org/need-prayer/. God is a God of second chances, and he is ready and willing to extend one to you today.

Second, if you are a follower of Christ, you need to know that what Daniel did here is the kind of work we need to do with those around us. We too need to be faithful in unfaithful times. And when God gives us the opportunity, we need to speak up and share the bad news in hopes that those we love will come to know the good news. Sometimes they will turn to him. Other times they won't. But after thirty years under Nebuchadnezzar, Daniel was faithful to do what he believed was right. He spoke up to share the truth when the opportunity presented itself. So let's get out there today and do the same.

—— **If you are a man who wants to live the last part of your life better than the first, you can declare that right now.** ——

ASK THIS

Do you need prayer? Or is there someone you want to pray for?

DO THIS

Go to the webpage I mentioned earlier, or seek a trusted friend or church member to pray for you. Or if you want to pray for someone, write down the person's first name, then pray.

PRAY THIS

God, I need you. Give me direction on how to be a better man in this next part of my life.

JOURNAL

ONE LAST CHANCE

WHEN YOU WORK FOR A MAN WHO THINKS HE'S GOD

"All this came upon King Nebuchadnezzar. At the end of twelve months he was walking on the roof of the royal palace of Babylon, and the king answered and said, 'Is not this great Babylon, which I have built by my mighty power as a royal residence and for the glory of my majesty?'"

Daniel 4:28–30

God had been warning Nebuchadnezzar for thirty years! He'd given him many warnings. The first warning came with a dream of his empire being destroyed. Next, three men were saved by God from the fury of the king's rage and were unscathed by a fiery furnace. And last, God gave him a final warning in a dream about his future. Daniel even pleaded with him, essentially saying, "You have done great, but you are not as great as God."

God warned and then waited for the king to turn to him. He warned and waited. You have to agree that God gave him a lot of time. After the last warning, God gave him another whole year. But again, we see that Nebuchadnezzar's selfishness had burrowed too deeply. We see in his statement above that he was intoxicated with his accomplishments, might, and majesty. His unredeemed mind was forever drunk on himself. He was resistant to God because, in his mind, he had become a god.

I see two applications of this text.

First, it speaks to those men who fear God but who work under the leadership of someone who doesn't fear God. This was Daniel's situation. If you are in this context, you need to learn to trust God's sovereignty. His provision will guide you through this time. Your job is to trust him and act in faith. As you do, he will speak through you and may even rescue you, just like he spoke through Daniel and rescued Shadrach, Meshach, and Abednego.

Your outcome may not be what you'd prefer. You might be stripped of your rights, religious practices, name, and even your reproductive organs. Yet you can endure with God's help. Daniel found a way to faithfully serve both Nebuchadnezzar and God over these thirty years. I am sure it was hard sometimes to understand how to do so. But this was his path. And who knows—it might be yours too.

Second, the text speaks about those who don't fear God but think they are gods. God is calling men to obedience. He gives them time to repent. He gives them way more time than we would give to an incompetent employee or a belligerent son. Why? Because he is far more patient than we are, which is why it's a good thing that you and I are not God!

But his patience does eventually come to an end. And on the other side is destruction for even the greatest of men, because no man is as mighty as God. What was about to happen to Nebuchadnezzar is a sobering warning for ungodly men.

Catch this, though: the applications are identical for both men. The man who fears God needs to let God be God. And the man who does not fear God needs to let God be God. So, dear brother, let God be God. Let him do his job today and do your best to get on board … or you may meet with imminent destruction.

—— You can endure with God's help. ——

ASK THIS

Are you letting God do his job or not?

DO THIS

Let God be God.

PRAY THIS

God, I confess you are God and I am not.

JOURNAL

GOD IS ALWAYS SPEAKING

"While the words were still in the king's mouth, there
fell a voice from heaven, 'O King Nebuchadnezzar,
to you it is spoken: The kingdom has departed from
you, and you shall be driven from among men, and
your dwelling shall be with the beasts of the field.
And you shall be made to eat grass like an ox, and
seven periods of time shall pass over you, until you
know that the Most High rules the kingdom of men
and gives it to whom he will.' Immediately the word
was fulfilled against Nebuchadnezzar."

Daniel 4:31–33

Sometimes people ask me what happens to those who are never exposed
to God's Word. I think Nebuchadnezzar is a great example.

Just because someone doesn't have a Bible in his hands or a church in
his area doesn't excuse him from believing. Nor does it mean God can't
reach him. God speaks to men in more than one way, and definitely not
always in the way we expect him to. God calls to all men over a lifetime
using a variety of means: events, dreams, circumstances, and his people.
He presents these invitations to us faithfully, giving us numerous opportunities to believe, which is precisely what happened here.

Without a Bible or church in sight, Nebuchadnezzar was given dreams, visions, explanations, miracles, and warnings from God and his people—yet he rejected them all. But a moment will come when God himself will speak and confront the king personally. There will come a reckoning.

This is the truth for all men, even today. God declares to all people that he is God, even if they have no Bible or local church. He did it this way long before the Bible was ever printed or churches (or even synagogues) had been established. And definitely long before your denomination ever existed.

God gave Nebuchadnezzar multiple opportunities to believe, even though he was surrounded by pagan ideas, politics, and idols. Which I think pretty much excludes us all from any excuse, because God can and will reveal himself in more than one way.

The question is not "Is God speaking?" The better question is "Are you listening?" Are you hearing God and heeding his voice? Because on the last day, all men will meet with the terror of his mighty voice. And you want to make sure that it's not the first time you've heeded it, because at that moment, it's going to be too late.

The question is not "Is God speaking?" The better question is "Are you listening?"

ASK THIS

Are you obeying God's voice?

DO THIS

Listen to his voice through people, dreams, circumstances, and Scripture today.

PRAY THIS

God, I want to hear and listen to your voice.

JOURNAL

GOD IS ALWAYS SPEAKING

DON'T PLAY GOD— JUST FOLLOW HIM

"At the end of the days I, Nebuchadnezzar, lifted my eyes to heaven, and my reason returned to me, and I blessed the Most High, and praised and honored him who lives forever, for his dominion is an everlasting dominion, and his kingdom endures from generation to generation; all the inhabitants of the earth are accounted as nothing, and he does according to his will among the host of heaven and among the inhabitants of the earth; and none can stay his hand or say to him, 'What have you done?' At the same time my reason returned to me, and for the glory of my kingdom, my majesty and splendor returned to me. My counselors and my lords sought me, and I was established in my kingdom, and still more greatness was added to me. Now I, Nebuchadnezzar, praise and extol and honor the King of heaven, for all his works are right and his ways are just; and those who walk in pride he is able to humble."

Daniel 4:34–37

I have two questions about this text.

First, was this a declaration of Nebuchadnezzar's salvation? He'd been out in the wilderness living like a madman for seven years. He came to his senses, returned to the throne, and wrote this passage. Does it mean he got saved? The simple answer is that we don't know, because this is the end of the narrative about him. It's all we have. We have seen him flip-flop before, and we have no real evidence that this confession took him anywhere.

What we know is that Nebuchadnezzar is portrayed as one of the greatest villains in the Bible. His wickedness is referenced in six books of the Bible, and he is described as vehemently opposed to God every time.

But here's the deal: whether this king was saved or not is not the primary issue. The bigger issue is this: Do *you* believe that God is God? Will you surrender to him and let him be your King, Savior, and Lord? That's the only question that matters. It's the only one that needs to be answered.

You can do that right now. You can make that decision today and stop fighting with the God of the universe. You can proclaim him King of Kings and Lord of Lords and let him lead your life today. But you will have to surrender doing life your way and agree to do it his way—forever.

Will you surrender to God and let him be your King, Savior, and Lord?

If you are ready to do that, I would love for you to reach out to me. You can contact me directly at the following webpage or via the QR code to the right: https://beresolute.org/contact/.

Here's the second question I have about today's passage: What was Daniel doing for those seven years? If he was the number-two guy, and if number one lost his mind and went stumbling around out in the wilderness with wild animals, what was Daniel doing? He wouldn't even have to march on the capital to take over the throne. It was his for the taking. He could've just declared himself king, set all the Jewish people free, and financed the rebuilding of Jerusalem. But he didn't.

The Bible doesn't tell us what he was doing, but I have a guess. I think Daniel was being faithful. He was being obedient. He was not taking matters into his own hands. He was serving faithfully while God was teaching the king a timeless lesson. The lesson was that Nebuchadnezzar wasn't number one. No person can *be* number one. We never see Daniel try to play God. He just faithfully followed him.

That's the lesson for today: don't play God—just follow God.

ASK THIS

How have you been playing God? Are you ready to stop and surrender to God?

DO THIS

If you are ready, reach out to me today.

PRAY THIS

God, I surrender all to you.

JOURNAL

DON'T PLAY GOD—JUST FOLLOW HIM

JOURNAL

ADDITIONAL
LINED PAGES

STRONG AS A MAN OF GOD

With Scripture, prayers, and actionable ideas, this devotional series from Bible teacher Vince Miller challenges you to stand up for your faith and draw closer to God. Each devotion reminds you that even in the hard moments and the stressful days, God is with you to strengthen, help, and provide.